A Year of Weekly Inspiration for Success:
Quotes & Notes
Ideal for Entrepreneurs

Copyright © 2020 Kathy Heshelow
All rights reserved.

(ISBN on back of book)

Welcome to inspiration and motivation!

This book, which can also serve as a journal, offers you weekly inspiration through quotes from me or public domain quotes of amazing people on success.

I ask a GUIDING QUESTION after each quote to help you with your own goals and success.

There is room at the bottom of the page and on the facing page for your own notes, inspiration, or ideas that may come to you.

I hope you find the book useful and enjoyable!

- Kathy Heshelow

Week 1

There is nothing more satisfying that having a goal or dream, taking action steps towards that goal, and then achieving it!
-Kathy Heshelow

WHAT IS YOUR GOAL?

Week 2

It is true that if you think you CAN accomplish something, you will. If you think you CAN'T, you won't. So much starts with your mindset.
-Kathy Heshelow

IS YOUR MINDSET IN THE RIGHT PLACE?

Week 3

The little phrase "take action" is monumental in the end.
-Kathy Heshelow

ARE YOUR MINI ACTION STEPS IN PLACE TO REACH YOUR GOALS - AND ARE YOU DOING THEM EACH DAY?

Week 4

"As long as you live, keep learning how to live."
- Seneca (4 BC-65 AD)

LEARN EVERY DAY. TAKE ON NEW SKILLS NEEDED FOR YOUR GOAL.

Week 5

"Throw off your worries when you throw off your clothes at night"
– Napolean Bonaparte (1769-1821)

LEARN TO CONTROL STRESS & LEAVE IT BEHIND. IT ONLY HINDERS YOU.

Week 6

"What is not started will never get finished."
– Johann Wolfgang von Goethe (1749-1832)

HAVE YOU BEGUN TAKING ACTION TOWARDS YOUR GOAL?

Week 7

"The way to get started is to quit talking and begin doing."
- Walt Disney

IT'S EXCITING TO HAVE A GOAL, BUT YOU HAVE TO MAKE IT HAPPEN! ARE YOU?

Week 8

"The less one has to do, the less one finds to do it in."
- Lord Chesterfield (1694-1773)

TIME MANAGEMENT OF YOUR TASKS IS KEY. SET SPECIFIC TIMES ON YOUR GOALS WITHOUT DISTRACTION.

Week 9

"The beginning is the most important part of the work."
-Plato 428 BC

HAVE YOU PLANNED HOW TO REACH YOUR GOAL, AND HAVE YOUR FIRST ACTION STEPS IN PLACE?

Week 10

"For a man to conquer himself is the first and noblest of victories."
-Plato 428 BC

HAVE YOU CONQUERED FEARS OF REACHING YOUR GOALS? ARE YOU WORKING TO IMPROVE YOUR WEAKNESSES?

Week 11

A person
who never made a mistake
never tried anything new.
- Albert Einstein

DON'T BE AFRAID OF MAKING MISTAKES! EVERYONE DOES.

Week 12

"Whatever you are, be a good one."
- Abraham Lincoln

WORK AT BEING YOUR BEST.

Week 13

"Whatever the mind can conceive and believe, the mind can achieve."
– Dr. Napoleon Hill (born 1883)

I RE-READ HILL'S "THINK & GROW RICH" EVERY YEAR. SO INSPIRING. WHAT INSPIRES YOU?

Week 14

"Opportunity is missed by most people because it is dressed in overalls and looks like work."
– Thomas Edison (1847-1931)

DON'T BE AFRAID TO WORK HARD NOW, TO ATTAIN FREEDOM LATER.

Week 15

"I find that the harder I work, the more luck I seem to have."
- Thomas Jefferson
(1743-1826)

Week 16

"Genius is one percent inspiration and ninety-nine percent perspiration."
- Thomas Edison (1847-1931)

DON'T GIVE UP ON YOUR DREAM OR GOAL!

Week 17

"It is better to be alone than in bad company."
- George Washington
(1732-1799)

DO YOU SURROUND YOURSELF WITH LIKE-MINDED, GOAL-ORIENTED PEOPLE (NOT NAY-SAYERS)?

Week 18

The secret of getting ahead is getting started. The secret of getting started is breaking your complex overwhelming tasks into small manageable tasks, and then starting on the first one.
-Mark Twain (1835-1910)

Week 19

"I am not afraid. I was born to do this."
- Joan of Arc (1412-1432)

ARE YOU DETERMINED AND FEARLESS?

Week 20

You can do this! Do something every single day towards your goal. Be consistent, and you will see results!

- Kathy Heshelow

Week 21

Success seems to be connected with action. Successful people keep moving. They make mistakes, but they don't quit.
- Conrad Hilton (born 1887)

Week 22

"A superior man is modest in his speech, but exceeds in his actions."

-Confucius (551 BC-479 BC)

Week 23

Entrepreneurship is living a few years of your life like most people won't
so you can spend the rest of your life like most people can't.

— Anonymous

Week 24

"Knowing is not enough; we must apply. Willing is not enough; we must do."
- Johann Wolfgang von Goethe (1749-1832)

Week 25

"Do not dwell in the past, do not dream of the future, concentrate the mind on the present moment."
- Buddha (551 BC-479 BC

ARE YOU FOCUSING ON THE NOW, ON WHAT YOU NEED TO DO TO ATTAIN YOUR GOAL?

Week 26

Focusing like a laser on your tasks and habits each day, without distractions, is what will propel you forward.
- Kathy Heshelow

ARE YOU REMOVING DISTRACTIONS WITH THE TIME YOU HAVE TO WORK TOWARDS YOUR GOAL?

Week 27

"To keep the body in good health is a duty ... otherwise we shall not be able to keep our mind strong and clear."
- Buddha

ARE YOU EXERCISING, EATING WELL, GETTING SLEEP FOR YOUR OPTIMAL SELF? DON'T NEGLECT THIS!

Week 28

Don't be afraid of your goals. Figure out how you can reach them, make your plan, and then just do it. You will not regret it.
- Kathy Heshelow

Week 29

"The golden rule for every businessman is this: Put yourself in your customer's place."
- Orison Swett Marden (1848–1924)

Week 30

"If you cannot do great things, do small things in a great way."
-Napoleon Hill (born 1883)

Week 31

"Nothing can stop the man with the right mental attitude from achieving his goal; nothing on earth can help the man with the wrong mental attitude."
- Thomas Jefferson

SO VERY TRUE! HAVE YOU DEVELOPED THE RIGHT ATTITUDE?

Week 32

"Beware of missing chances; otherwise it may be altogether too late some day"
- Franz Liszt (1811-1886)

IT IS NEVER TOO LATE TO START WORKING TOWARDS YOUR GOALS, OR HELPING OTHERS TOWARD THEIRS.

Week 33

"Most great people have attained their greatest success just one step beyond their greatest failure."
–Napoleon Hill

DON'T GIVE UP!

Week 34

"Experience is the teacher of all things."
- Julius Caesar (100-44 BC)

YOU LEARN, DEVELOP NEW SKILLS & GET EXPERIENCE THAT WILL SERVE YOU WELL AS YOU WORK TOWARD YOUR GOAL! WHAT HAVE YOU LEARNED SO FAR?

Week 35

Doing new things outside of your comfort zone is not to be feared, but welcomed. It might be uncomfortable at first, but forge on!
- Kathy Heshelow

Week 36

"Energy and persistence conquer all things."
- Benjamin Franklin

I LOVE THIS SIMPLE BUT POWERFUL STATEMENT! ARE YOU PERSISTENT?

Week 37

"Develop success from failures. Discouragement and failure are two of the surest stepping stones to success."
- Dale Carnegie (born 1888)

Week 38

"Do not take life too seriously. You will never get out of it alive."
- Elbert Hubbard (1859-1915)

ARE YOU ENJOYING YOUR JOURNEY? IT PASSES TOO QUICKLY NOT TO.

Week 39

"Don't judge each day by the harvest that you reap but by the seeds that you plant."
- Robert Louis Stevenson (1850-1894)

KEEP TAKING CONSISTENT ACTION TOWARDS YOUR GOALS!

Week 40

Develop your daily habits and works flows needed to attain your goals - and then do them consistently!
- Kathy Heshelow

Week 41

"Action is the foundational key to all success."
- Pablo Picasso (born 1881)

I REPEAT THIS THOUGHT OFTEN BECAUSE IT IS ONE THAT STOPS TOO MANY - ACTION! ARE YOU TAKING ACTION?

Week 42

"Follow your own star!"
-Dante Aligheri (1265-1321)

YOU CAN DO IT!

Week 43

"Obstacles are those frightful things you see when you take your eyes off your goal."
- Henry Ford (born 1863)

KEEP FOCUSED ON YOUR GOALS AND ATTAINING THEM!

Week 44

"The will to win, the desire to succeed, the urge to reach your full potential... these are the keys that will unlock the door to personal excellence.
- Confucius

Week 45

"Determine that the thing can and shall be done, and then we shall find the way."
- Abraham Lincoln

Week 46

"Success is a science; if you have the conditions, you get the result.'
- Oscar Wilde (1854-1900)

THERE IS REALLY NO MYSTERY. HAVE YOUR PLAN & HOW TO IMPLEMENT IT, THEN DO IT.

Week 47

"Success is not final; failure is not fatal: it is the courage to continue that counts."
– Winston Churchill (born 1874)

Week 48

"That some achieve great success, is proof to all that others can achieve it as well".
- Abraham Lincoln

BE INSPIRED BY OTHERS SUCCESS; WORK TO INSPIRE OTHERS!

Week 49

"Our goals can only be reached through a vehicle of a plan, in which we must fervently believe, and upon which we must vigorously act. There is no other route to success."

- Pablo Picasso (born 1881)

HE DISTILLS IT PERFECTLY! ARE YOU IMPLEMENTING YOUR PLAN VIGOROUSLY?

Week 50

"Success usually comes to those who are too busy to be looking for it."
– Henry David Thoreau (1817-1862)

MY WISH FOR YOU!

Week 51

"The greater the obstacle, the more glory in overcoming it."
- Moliere (1622-1673)

KEEP GOING THROUGH OBSTACLES, IF ENCOUNTERED. ARE ANY IN YOUR WAY?

Week 52

There are basically two types of people. People who accomplish things, and people who claim to have accomplished things. The first group is less crowded.
- Mark Twain (1835-1910)

YOU ARE IN THE FIRST GROUP- OR WILL BE!

www.ingramcontent.com/pod-product-compliance
Lightning Source LLC
Chambersburg PA
CBHW071423210526
45465CB00001B/501